Unsettling the Land

Suzanne Bellamy and Susan Hawthorne

Poems by Susan Hawthorne
Artwork by Suzanne Bellamy

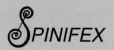

Spinifex Press Pty Ltd
PO Box 5270, North Geelong Vic 3215, Australia
PO Box 105, Mission Beach Qld 4852, Australia
women@spinifexpress.com.au
www.spinifexpress.com.au

First published by Spinifex Press, 2008. Reprinted 2023

Cover and book design by Deb Snibson.
Made and printed in Australia by Elikon Fine Printers.
Printed on Sovereign Silk, paper sources from sustainable forests.

National Library of Australia Cataloguing-in-Publication entry

Bellamy, Suzanne, 1948-2022
Hawthorne, Susan, 1951-
Unsettling the land / Suzanne Bellamy, Susan Hawthorne.

ISBN: 9781876756703

Australian poetry--21st century.

A821.408

We respectfully acknowledge the wisdom of Aboriginal and Torres Strait Islander peoples
and their custodianship of the lands and waterways. The Countries on which Spinifex
offices are situated are Djiru, Bunurong and Wurundjeri, Wadawurrung, Eora, and Noongar.

I saw three emus close to the water, disturbed 10 wild turkeys and put to flight any number of swans and native companions. In every little bay were pelicans by the score, singly, in pairs and by the hundred, mountain ducks in small bands, wood ducks, teal, blue cranes, black and white cranes by the hundred, white cranes by the thousand; ibises, both the ordinary kind and the all-white, in immense flocks, feeding in the long water-covered grass; great black shags.

— **George Ernest Morrison, 1881**

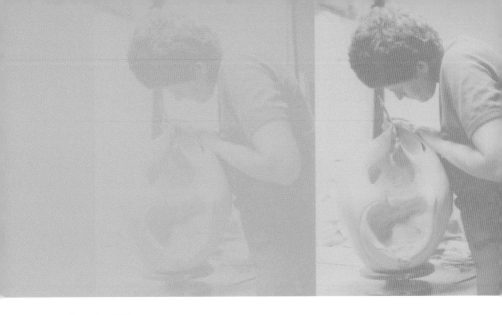

i Birdlife

What we have lost—
I grew beside the Murrumbidgee

its great highway of water
rumbling with us through each day

we played discovery—my brother
and I—imagining different lives

in which we were the first to name
certain corners, small islands

to memorialise ourselves—taking
no account in our teens of those

who'd been here so many
thousands of years. It is Wiradjuri

country, and on its banks sits the
town named for its crows.

Birds and water—a pair that
indicates vitality, a dynamic system,
a system

that changes season by season.
But in our unsettling of the land
we have

removed the seasons and the
birds—water flow is constant in the
irrigating

rivers—who ever heard of this before
the gouging out of dams, the
displacement

of earth to block water, to release it
at our want and whim and will.

Who will join with me to recall the
birds—the wetland birds back to

country—dancing brolgas, jabiru,
pelican and ibis—and the crow to

welcome back its dispossessed
cousins—a kind of Native Title for
the birds.

ii Drought, 1967

Mother, you and I walk across
the bladeless paddock, kicking dust

Oh, it breaks my heart so, you say—
a sentence exhaled with sadness.

Only now, do I really feel what
you said and how you said it.

I'm now a little older than you were
when dust and sighing mixed with

those words. It is thirty years and drought
is here again. There is something about

the air, the layering of dust, the loss
of grass, the particular sway of old

eucalypt branches and their browning
leaves. I feel my chest fill to breaking

I'd like to ask if you too think it's worse
this time—How long for recovery?

Every grief is simply layered
on top of the last. And the last.

Does the earth feel that way too?
How many griefs must we ply and

plough? How many layers before
the sadness breaks the earth's heart?

iii Flood, 1974

There's a roar that a river makes as
it breaks its banks–a sound that grumbles

deep into the body, *unearthly*, I think,
but earthly is what it is. We watch the

sun rise over the front paddock,
our bodies absorbing the flood's power,

a shuddering that is later taken up
by the muscles in a great release.

It is a day of contrasts: we children
sent to round up cattle, our unkitchened

mother bakes a loaf of bread, our father
is trapped in a tree for thirteen long hours

while we sleep, eat our mother's
bread, talk of the sky, the land,

the height of the river. Late afternoon
he is delivered in a boat, rescued by men

bearing sandwiches. None of us knew
of his ordeal until it was over. In the days

that follow we gauge the level of the river,
walk again the reduced banks, watch

the swirl of snag-driven water,
thrilling to the sudden birdlife.

in the

to

of

unseen water
hidden birdlife

unseen water
hidden birdlife

while we sleep, eat our mother's
bread, talk of the sky, the land

a shuddering that is later taken up
by the muscles in a great release

gauge the level of the ri...

ired banks, watch

ired banks, watch

Flood, 1974

they shape one another. Water seeps
through the soil, jumps down cliffs;

rocks bounce through streams,
clatter along shorelines.

In this time of separating land
from water, glove from hand

drought scrapes the surface
but it is our unsettling

that chops out the fingers
to claw at earth's innards.

iv Water, 2008

Water fits land like a glove fits a hand.
It follows the lay of the land, pools
in hollows and flows between inclines.
Water and land are intimate,

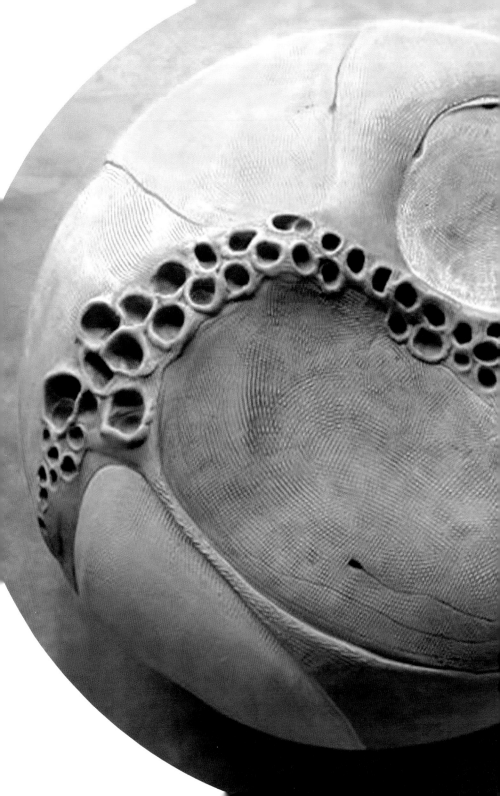

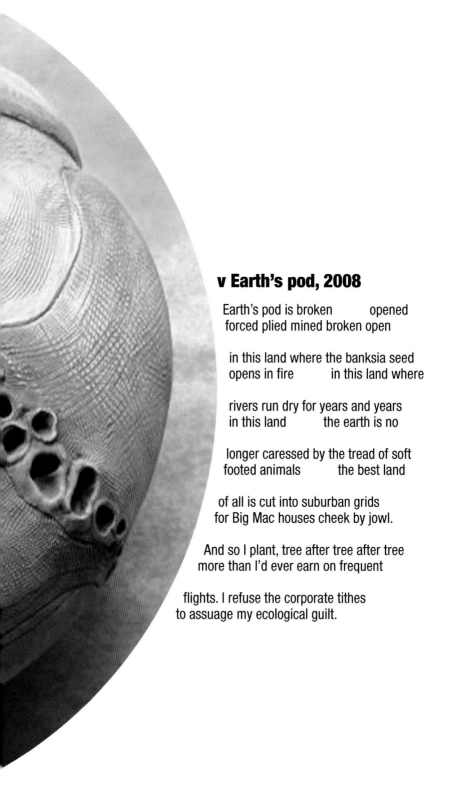

v Earth's pod, 2008

Earth's pod is broken   opened
forced plied mined broken open

    in this land where the banksia seed
    opens in fire   in this land where

    rivers run dry for years and years
    in this land   the earth is no

    longer caressed by the tread of soft
    footed animals   the best land

of all is cut into suburban grids
for Big Mac houses cheek by jowl.

    And so I plant, tree after tree after tree
    more than I'd ever earn on frequent

flights. I refuse the corporate tithes
to assuage my ecological guilt.

Suzanne Bellamy is a studio artist and writer working in mixed-media, clay, printmaking, canvas and performance. Developing a form she calls "the visual essay", she has in recent years combined ideas of text perception and image to explore the idea of visual thinking. Based in research on Gertrude Stein, Virginia Woolf and more recently early modernist ideas in Australian culture, she brings together notions of dual creativity and synaesthesia in the art of ideas. In parallel with these forms she has produced a large body of clay work and sculpture over many years in direct elemental relationship with earth fire water and air.

Susan Hawthorne is a writer, publisher and aerialist with a passion for creating poetry through the body and aerials that embodies text. She is inspired by ancient languages, the coding of culture, ecology, physics and the sheer audacity of contemporary feminists. Her collaboration with Suzanne inspired further poetry for the canvas. She is the author of two previous collections of poetry *Bird* (1999) and *The Butterfly Effect* (2005) and has another collection, *Earth's Breath* in preparation.

If you would like to know more about
Spinifex Press, write to us for a free catalogue, visit our
website or email us for further information
on how to subscribe to our monthly newsletter.

PO Box 105
Mission Beach Qld 4851
Australia

www.spinifexpress.com.au
women@spinifexpress.com.au

Many Spinifex titles are available as eBooks.
See the eBookstore on our website for more details.